Enzo Russo

Sicily
Land of Myth

Photography
Melo Minnella

arsenale et editrice

ENZO RUSSO
Sicily • Land of Myth

Photography
MELO MINNELLA

Translation from the Italian
Lemmy Caution

Printed by
EBS Editoriale Bortolazzi-Stei
Verona

First Edition
March 2003

Second reprint
December 2009

Arsenale Editore Srl
Via Ca' Nova Zampieri, 29
37057 San Giovanni Lupatoto (Vr)
www.arsenale.it

Arsenale Editrice © 2009

ISBN 978-88-7743-291-9

Page 1:
limestone statue of goddess suckling
*two children (*kourotrophos*), circa 550 BCE,*
from the southern necropolis of Megara
Iblea (Syracuse, Museo Archeologico
Regionale "P. Orsi").

Page 2:
small Maranello lakes,
under the promontory at Tindari.

Contents

ANCIENT
AND MEDIEVAL SICILY

IF THE ETRUSCANS' EXPANSIONIST policies, great artistic ability and cult of the dead might make us think of them as the Egyptians of Italy, then Sicily could be considered the Atlantis of the Mediterranean. Not the Atlantis dreamt of by philosophers or invented by ancient sailors, but a real Atlantis, able to fascinate and mesmerise entire populations and the greats of history who conquered, inhabited, exploited and enriched the island, and who left behind traces that were layered over traces left by preceding greats. Peoples and historical figures who, through greed or love, turned Sicily into a myth.

SOMEONE ONCE SAID that without writing there is no history. This is only partly true. We know very little about the Sicanians, Siculians or Elymians, and nothing at all about those who came before; but what they left behind communicates in a language that is quite different from writing. In the grottos of Addaura which look out towards the sea from the massif of Monte Pellegrino, Late Palaeolithic human figures etched onto rock have been used for many thousands of years in a fascinating dance ritual. Graffiti and tombs. The necropolis of Pantalica, the largest on the island, is overwhelming in the silence of sunset, demanding respect and provoking a sense of dread. Unlike the Sicanians who cremated their dead, the Siculians buried their loved ones, consigning them to the earth and memory.

ON THE OTHER HAND, the mysterious Sesians of Pantelleria did not consign their dead to the earth, but to volcanic stone. Five thousand years ago they built enormous mounds called *sese* using the only materials available to them on the island, and all around the base of these mounds they dug out little tunnels which quickly enlarged to form a mortuary. The largest of these, the so-called "*Sese* of the Kings", is six metres high and twelve metres wide. Who were the Sesians? And more to the point, how did they get this far? These are questions you cannot help but ask yourself as you contemplate this enormous mound of basalt rock in a wild, almost deserted landscape. Historically, Sicily was first colonised when the Phoenicians arrived on the western part of the island and the Greeks on the eastern shores. The former, who were merchants rather than conquerors, might well have founded a second Carthage had the more enterprising and combative Greeks allowed them. Ancient Mozia, now San Pantaleo, one of the islands of Stagnone just south of Trapani, is an extremely fascinating if not spectacular trace. A submerged road once linked the island to the mainland. The road, built to stop the ox-driven carts from sinking into the mud and slime, still exists. The small island was an economic bridgehead, and must have been extraordinarily busy with ships and people at the time. Still extant is the dry-dock area, a large, dark pool along the seaside which allowed ships to be brought in during high tide so that their keels could be worked on. The rustic villa belonging to the Whitakers, who owned Mozia and dabbled in excavation work, is also still extant. The villa is now a pleasant and comprehensive country museum containing many finds from the area, which have all been catalogued by the Whitakers, the English equivalent of the Gattopardi family.

BUT THE MOST EXTRAORDINARY remains are those pertaining to Greek religion. From a high ridge of light-coloured rock, the

Concordia temple faces onto the Agrigento valley, enthralling the passing motorists now just as, twenty-five centuries ago, it enchanted travellers and pilgrims who came to pay homage to their Hellenic gods. More than Athens', the Acropolis of ancient Akragas (Agrigento) helps us appreciate how closely linked this privileged *locus* of the city-state was to daily life. Here the citizens paid daily homage to the gods, but above all it was here that they met, discussed and made their decisions. The archaeological walk, which sets off from the temple, transmits a sense of the political and moral domination exerted by the religious buildings over the city which, according to Pindar, was "the most beautiful ever built by mortal man".

THE REMAINS OF SELINUNTE are no less striking. The Doric colony of Megara's city walls are still impressive if not because of their height, which has been eroded by the passing of time, then because of their breadth and width. Here, just as in Agrigento, there is a concentration of temples, which originally made the city one of the island's main pilgrim destinations.

Most of the temples have since been sacked or destroyed by time. Some, in fact, are now merely known by a letter of the alphabet, it having been impossible to determine which god they were originally dedicated to. The most impressive is the so-called "G" Temple, whose floor plan, larger than that of the Parthenon and the Basilica at Paestum, constitutes the largest ever for a Greek temple.

NATURALLY, THIS RELIGIOUS COMPLEX was more an exception than the rule. Often shrines dedicated to Olympian gods were secluded in the countryside or constituted the heart of the city, where they formed its central focus. One such case in point is the sanctuary dedicated to Venus at Erice, with its sublime view of the Trapani sea. An exemplary city, Erice is a sumptuously bound book of Sicilian history that can be leafed through as you walk through the streets. From the cyclopean walls, probably built by the Elymians, the city's founders, to the 19th century buildings, the island's history can be seen in the *palazzi* and castles, in the barely-visible ruins and archaeological finds. Though the ancient houses are not intact, they have nonetheless conserved a

good portion of their original spirit, thanks to the fact that the complex was built on top of a hill with extremely steep sides, which made it impossible to construct modern buildings in the vicinity (which, unfortunately, happened in Agrigento).

NONE OF THIS, HOWEVER, can compare with the Doric temple of Segesta, the way it rises apparently out of nowhere for those travellers expecting the usual landscape of little villas, enclosures, stalls and flocks of tourists. Like the temple of Concordia, its essential structure is still in one piece. Solitary, rising up in the open countryside, protected by an almost perfect silence, it suddenly comes into view as you round a bend, surrounded by fields of corn, poppies or wild grass, depending on the season. A spectacle so simple that it is shocking and enthralling, able to move you if you have the courage to let yourself go, even just a little.

AS YOU WALK UP an unsurfaced road you come to a theatre. Albeit small, the acoustics are perfect. And in the background you can make out the grey, almost menacing mountains.

Obviously, this is not the Taormina theatre, with its magnificent view of the beautiful and legendary stretch of sea and its backdrop of the unpredictable and authoritarian Etna. Nor is it the daunting theatre of Syracuse, which is still used to stage the same plays it was originally built for. But this is only one of the many treasures of what was once the richest and most powerful *polis* of the Mediterranean, and Italy's second most important city after Rome in terms of archaeological and architectural wealth.

NEITHER THE CARTHAGINIANS nor the Athenians ever managed to annex the city; in fact, under the ironclad and ingenious rule of Dionysius the Elder the city subjugated virtually the entire island and pushed its influence as far afield as the Adriatic, where it founded the city of Ancona. While for the Punic city-state it was simply a defeat that did not compromise its increasing power, the defeat at Nicaea constituted the beginning of the end for Athens. An attack by a strong army, too sure of its own means, came to a shuddering halt before the sophisticated defence system put together by the Sicilian city-state, the fulcrum of which was

Castello Eurialo. The only section of the castle still extant is the underground section, which it is believed was once directly linked via a secret underground passage to the city many kilometres away. Seven thousand prisoners were locked up in the damp Latomie, where they awaited their death.

THE MOST INCREDIBLE of these tufa grottoes, which are almost completely undamaged and parts of which can be visited, is the so-called "Orecchio di Dionisio" (literally, "Dionysus' Ear"). Legend has it that thanks to the very strange configuration of the enormous cavern, the tyrant was able to hear each and every word pronounced by the prisoners. The expert guides know exactly where to stand so that when they click their fingers they can be heard by all the visitors in the cave, even if they are tens of metres away; the noise continues to be amplified as it ricochets off the curved walls, multiplying and increasing in volume as it goes.

STRANGELY ENOUGH, and contrary to normal custom, the Romans have left very little in Sicily. This is perhaps due to the fact that Sicily

was already extremely well developed, and the Romans' pragmatic approach left little room for the destruction of what they deemed useful or the construction of what they considered to be superfluous. Considering the fact that their domination was the longest in Sicily's history, it is nonetheless bizarre that so little has remained. An archaeologist from another planet who knew very little about Italian history would consider Rome's impact on the island to be negligible. There are very few exceptions, and almost none of these are of any artistic or architectural interest barring the theatre at Tindari, which was originally built by the Greeks and then rebuilt by the Romans, and the famous Villa del Casale, with its extraordinary, and extraordinarily well-preserved, mosaics.

All of this begs a question. Who does a country really belong to? From a legal point of view, the answer is simple. But what about from an historical or moral point of view? Does it belong to those who have inhabited it longer than others, or to those who have left more traces of themselves? Or to the last occupiers? Or to those whose blood flows in the veins of its people? In this sense, Sicily is truly exemplary. The "real" Sicilian could in effect only have existed in some proto-historic period. Since then there has been a constant succession of immigrants, where each dominant people, after having left behind colonies and genetic material, was in its turn dominated by another people. Who exactly were the Sicilians dominated by the Bourbons if not an inextricable mixture of Sicanians, Phoenicians, Greeks, Byzantines, Arabs, Normans and so on, including the odd wayward traveller and pirate, not to mention many others?

No country except for Sicily gives one the impression of belonging to everyone. And when a country is particularly rich in historical memory, it belongs (historically and morally) to humanity itself.

THE BYZANTINES, THE ARABS and then the Normans, left quite different traces compared to the Greeks and Romans. It is curious to note how the three have combined harmoniously, forming a unique style that can be found in Sicily alone. The *duomo* at Monreale is a sublime example. The church's structure, its portal, cloister, portico and mosaics covering over six thousand square metres, are a symbolic synthesis of different races, cultures and traditions, expressing a sense of the mystic and divine that is superior to the spirit of each of the various religions that followed and supplanted each other in Sicily. It is no exaggeration to say that Monreale deserves to be seen even if you do not plan to see any other part of the island. Its cloister is unique in the world: it has two hundred and twenty-eight columns, some smooth and unadorned, others painted or covered in mosaics, some inlaid and others still engraved. The capitals are Corinthian, but the classical ornamental motifs of this particular style are embellished with little human figures. It is clear that no one intended to follow a single artistic genre or style. The *duomo*, which Guglielmo II of Altavilla had built and then donated to the Benedictine monks, obviously aimed to make proudly explicit the concept of the universal nature of Sicilian culture.

THE ARAB PRESENCE is more evident in the *palazzi* and churches; sometimes the Arab style stands alone, at other times it is mixed with Norman elements, and this can most clearly be seen in Palermo. In the church of San Giovanni degli Eremiti, for example, with its Islamic cupolas and a small, delightful cloister. In the castle of Zisa, in the Palermo Cuba and the so-called Little Cuba of Vicari. The prevalence of the "North men" can be felt in the enchanting church of Martorana, and is much more evident in the cathedral, in the Palatine Chapel and the Palazzo dei Normanni, where, however, the magnificence of the Sala dei Re Ruggero is more reminiscent of an emirate's royal palace than that of an "emperor born and bred in Europe".

The cathedral deserves a chapter of its own. The inattentive tourist might, from afar, mistake it for a manor house because of its turrets and ramparts. Its history goes way back. It was originally a palaeo-Christian church, then a Byzantine church under the direct control of Constantinople; then it became the city's main mosque before being converted once again to a Christian church by the Normans, who embellished and extended it, ultimately providing its current form. A tormented history, therefore, and yet there are very few historical monuments on the island that have not been restructured by different owners and re-adapted for domestic, military or administrative use. Despite all these changes, however, the cathedral has always maintained its role as the city's main sacred building. The Cefalù *duomo* has an even more military aspect, with its crenellated turrets topped by two unequal pyramids, which make it look like an elegant fortress. This image is reinforced by the blocks of light stone with which it was built, and which are very unusual for religious buildings.

THE NORMAN PRESENCE (and to a much lesser extent the Byzantine presence) can clearly be seen in the castles, which, in the Middle Ages, had the same function as city walls did in the classical period. Castles were intended to protect the lord, who no longer had soldiers enough to guard the walls of an entire city – the walls themselves had also virtually disappeared during the long Roman domination, when the Empire certainly didn't fear any form of attack so far from the borders of the Empire. Castles in Sicily come in all shapes and sizes.

Some are almost completely intact, others have been reduced to mere rubble where even the *genius loci* has disappeared, and some have such an obscure history that even tireless local historians cannot piece it together.

LIKE THE TEMPLE at Segesta, Ursino castle in Catania comes suddenly into view as you approach from the slum-like cityscape. Though re-adapted and modified, it has maintained its noble aspect thanks to the empty mote dominating a *piazza* surrounded by old *palazzi* of the city's middle class. It once faced onto the sea, which has been forced back over the centuries by eruptions from Etna and subsequent landfills. Castello Maniace in Syracuse is magnificent and worthy of hosting a royal court (as it has in fact done in the past). It is the work of the great Riccardo da Lentini, and was named in honour of the Byzantine general, Giorgio Maniace, who had fought against the Saracens. This fortified palace was built by Frederick II, who was considered by the Vatican to be a sort of baptised sultan because of the oriental nature of his lifestyle, his scientific interests and above all because of his ill-disguised avarice

when it came to Church donations (Norman Catholics had never held back when it came to offering donations and privileges to the Church).

Minute and unique in its genre, the ancient fortress of Aci Castello is built on lava which must once have been completely surrounded by sea and that a subsequent eruption has turned into a promontory.

In that part of the Ionian coast it is Etna that defines as it wills the limits between sea and land. From the windowsill of one of the very few windows in the castle you can see the Saracen Coast, Etna and the stacks of Aci Trezza, which, according to myth, an already-blinded Polyphemus hurled against the fleeing Ulysses, who had dared laugh at him.

FOR REASONS OF DEFENCE, however, fortresses were not always built on top of steep cliffs. Take Castello di Lombardia in Enna, for example, which dominates the highest province in Italy. Its name derives from the garrison of Lombardy mercenaries who had come to protect the area for a short period of time, but who eventually settled in the city. It is large enough to have housed a small army, and is now used for open-air performances. Its keep, which is about thirty metres high, commands such a view of the island that it must have allowed the garrison to spot approaching enemies several days in advance.

The same can be said for the castles of Butera (once an important military and political centre) – Mussomeli, extremely beautiful and suggestive, and Mazzarino, which holds an exemplary position and survived the 1693 earthquake virtually intact. Unlike the preceding, however, the delightful and well-preserved castle of Falconara was almost built on the beach, which was also the original location of the castle of Ursino. This latter is so much slighter and less forbidding than Falconara that it almost appears to be a recent building, almost an architectural imitation commissioned by a capricious millionaire with a view to surprising his guests.

THE CASTLE OF SPERLINGA is a case unto itself. It is built on an enormous block of tufa in the small town of the same name near Enna. The oldest houses have in fact been excavated from this crumbly rock,

just like the "first floor" of this fortress and the staircase leading to the upper floors. On this floor one room leads directly to another – the prison, the grain stores and a large room originally intended, perhaps, for important meetings or huge banquets, on whose tufa walls stonemasons notched out the torch-brackets. The fortress proper was then built above these cavern-rooms. Over the main entrance gate an engraving reminds us that the small town was the only place in all of Sicily to have offered asylum to the fleeing French during the Sicilian Vespers. The text reads: *Quod Siculis placuit sola Sperlinga negavit.* A proud declaration of dissent with the Sicilians rebelling against the Angevin domination, certainly one of the harshest and despicable in the island's troubled history.

AS HEAVY WEAPONRY began to assert itself, castles became less and less important; as a building devised principally for military purposes, the castle offered little in terms of comfort or luxury. Hence began the construction of large *palazzi,* the earliest examples of which were rather dour and scantily decorated, not surprisingly considering the fact

that they descended directly from the castle model. Gradually, however, they became less weighty and brighter. An excellent example of this new trend in "baronial" architecture is Palazzo Steri (Chiaramonte, Palermo), completed in the late 14th century and decorated with paintings on religious, warlike and mythological themes that are unique in Sicily.

THE PERIOD THAT WENT from the construction of Palazzo Steri to the two wings of large Art Nouveau villas that lined Via Libertà (opened in the early 20th century) and destroyed during the architectural "sack of Palermo" was one of great ferment. Much was built in terms of both city and country dwellings where barons and viceroys, wealthy landowners and princes sought tangible outward show of their status and power. This was the beginning of the Gattopardi era, which was to last three or four centuries. But that is another story.

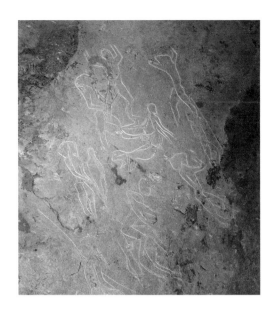

PREHISTORY

Those peoples who have no writing are condemned to eternal silence. Their voice is reduced to a few buildings and those artifacts that successive civilisations and the millennia have allowed to survive. It is difficult, if not impossible, to decipher the real meaning behind the Pantelleria *sesi*, which are enormous mounds of stone. Or even to imagine the funerals, the liturgical rites, the pain or the prayers held at the immense Pantalica necropolis. Or to understand what led Paleolithic man to cover the cave walls at Addaura with engravings, perhaps working by torchlight. Perhaps he worked alone, or perhaps accompanied by his contemporaries, mesmerised or even frightened by his skill.

Above: wall carvings in the Addaura grotto (Palermo).

Right: view of a wall from the Pantalica necropolis (Syracuse).

Pages 16-17: bronze Age village atop Punta Milazzese, island of Panarea (Messina).

THE PHOENICIANS

Imperialists without an empire. This is what the Phoenicians were during their era. Cities, colonies, ships, commerce and above all incredible bravery and complete indifference to limits, whether they were geographical or mythological. They had no sense of nation, or perhaps they didn't believe in the concept and thought it was superfluous or even counter-productive in terms of their aims. They were entrepreneurs, merchants, explorers, and not politicians, philosophers or soldiers. Tyre, Sidon, Byblos and other main cities were all independent, the maritime republics of antiquity.

Right:
Phoenician votive stele, from the Mozia trophet (Trapani), 6th-5th century BCE (Mozia-Trapani, Museo Whitaker).

Following page: remains of the Punic-Roman city of Solunto, Santa Flavia (Palermo).

GREEK COLONISATION

Like Magna Graecia, Sicily was a centre of Greek culture, and its cities, even though they were politically independent from their Greek counterparts, conserved their fundamental principle: the *polis* was compact and conservative, hegemonically controlling its own territory, and was often in contrast with other city-states. It was thanks to these cities that the Phoenicians' expansionist policies were thwarted, and the two civilisations had to share the island until the Romans arrived.

Right: decorated polychrome skyphoide pyx by the Lipari Painter showing Hera between Aphrodite and Eros, *290-270 BCE (Lipari-Messina, Museo Archeologico Regionale "Luigi Bernabò Brea").*

Following page: statue of a young man in tunic dress, known as the Mozia Ephebe *(Trapani), second quarter of the 5th century BCE (Mozia-Trapani, Museo Whitaker).*

THE GREEK TEMPLES

Like the cathedral of Christianity, the Greek temple was a place where mortals met with their god, but unlike Christian churches, which were the exclusive domain of worship, the temples were surrounded by markets, feasting and meetings. They were the real symbol of the city, and in fact while the most important European churches vied with the magificence of the palaces and castles of power (often losing the "battle"), the Greek temples are almost all extant while none of the buildings representing "temporal power" have survived. The primitive scheme was very simple: a sacred area, almost always woodland, contained a window-less cell (to highlight "mystery" through darkness) with a roof with double slopes made of wood and clay tiles. The roof was held up by columns which were originally made of brick, then painted wood and finally marble. It was only later that the so-called peripteral temple came about, where the cell was surrounded by a broad portico. The body of the columns was made up of cylindrical elements placed on top of each other (known as "drums"), which were lifted into position with a series of complex machines and rope. The final section, the capital, was either Doric (squared), Ionic (with swirling motifs) or Corinthian (elegantly ornate). The large stone architraves of the roof were then positioned on the capitals.

Pages 24-25:
the Segesta chora with its Doric peripteral temple, 430-420 BCE.

Right:
temple F, known as the Temple of Concord, Valle dei Templi (Agrigento), 440-430 BCE.

Pages 26-27:
the Segesta (Trapani) theatre, probably built as early as the mid-6th century BCE.

GODS AND DIVINITIES

The pantheon of gods on the island was the same as the Greek pantheon, and their temples were dedicated to the same divinities. We know nothing about the religions of earlier inhabitants – the Sesians, Sicanes, Elymians or Siculians. Even the Sicilian Carthaginians quite naturally worshiped the gods of their homeland – Baal, Amon (who was offered human sacrifice) and later Tanit (the supreme female deity).

Right:
the Landoline Aphrodite, marble copy found in Syracuse, first half of 2nd century BCE (Syracuse, Museo Archeologico Regionale "P. Orsi").

Following page: painted terracotta slab with Gorgon, 570 BCE, from the Athenaion temenos, Ortigia (Syracuse, Museo Archeologico Regionale "P. Orsi").

ROMAN DOMINATION

With the conquest of Syracuse in 212 BCE, Rome completed the occupation of Sicily, which was the first province of the Empire. Apart from Verres' misuse of public funds, immortalised by Cicero, Rome administered the province well and applied reasonable laws that had already been tried and tested in Rome for centuries, and that would continue to do so for five hundred years.

Right:
Taormina theatre (Messina), built during the Hellenic period. The building currently visible is in fact an Imperial reworking. The original structure was considerably enlarged, and covered the remains of a small Hellenic temple.

Page 32:
Roman sarcophagus in the crypt of the Palermo cathedral.

Page 33:
Roman basilica, or meeting room, in Tindari (Messina), late Imperial period.

Page 34:
the "bikini" room, Villa del Casale, Piazza Armerina (Enna).

Page 35:
hunter being attacked by a lioness in the corridor known as The Great Hunt, Villa del Casale, Piazza Armerina (Enna).

ARAB DOMINATION

No conquerer has ever loved his conquered land as much as the Arabs did Sicily. Sicily was conquered very gradually over a 75-year period; Arab domination then lasted about 170 years, before the arrival of the Normans. Historically speaking, this was not a very long time, and yet the Arabs left an indelible mark on the island's architecture, language, art, agriculture and cuisine. In terms of architecture, the Arabs' contribution was more subtle and penetrating than might be thought. While Zisa and Cuba are evident and almost monumental traces of the Arab art of construction, there is no ancient Sicilian town that does not bear some trace of Arab intervention. There are more than two hundred Arab gardens in Pantelleria, and Morish friezes and embellishments, albeit faded, can be found in noble *palazzi* and public buildings which were built well after the Arab conquest. From wells covered by small cupolas of stone and chalk, which, despite their rarity, are still extant in the inland country areas, to poor housing with vaulted roofs that were still being built in the early post-WWII years.

Left:
remains of the Arab fort of Mazzalaccar, on the banks of Lake Arancio, Sambuca di Sicilia (Agrigento).

Pages 38-39:
the Rabato quarter of Sutera (Caltanissetta), with its Arab layout.

ARAB ART

Unlike the Romans, the Arabs left behind an extraordinary artistic heritage on the island. The church of Martorana and the Monreale duomo are probably the most noble examples of what was later defined as the Arab-Norman-Byzantine style. Another example of this magic mixture of styles is San Giovanni degli Eremiti in Palermo, whose cupolas are reminiscent of a mosque. In the deft and marvellously ornate cloisters there is all the beauty of Arab culture, of their daily life, in sharp contrast with the megalithic solemnity of the Greek temples and the engineering mastery of the Romans. Obviously, the Arabs aimed to please the eye and privileged the freshness of the garden, an earthly example of what could be expected after death for those who lived according to the strictures of the Koran or who fell fighting for their faith.

Right:
the rectangular, compact façade of Cuba, Palermo, at the summit of which there is an Arab inscription which bears the name of the founding king, William II, and the date (1180). A marvellous example of Fatima architecture, the building was originally surrounded by an artificial lake surrounded by a garden, and was used as a pleasure dome for rest and "holidays". It was so famous that Boccaccio set one of his Decameron stories here (Day V, 6).

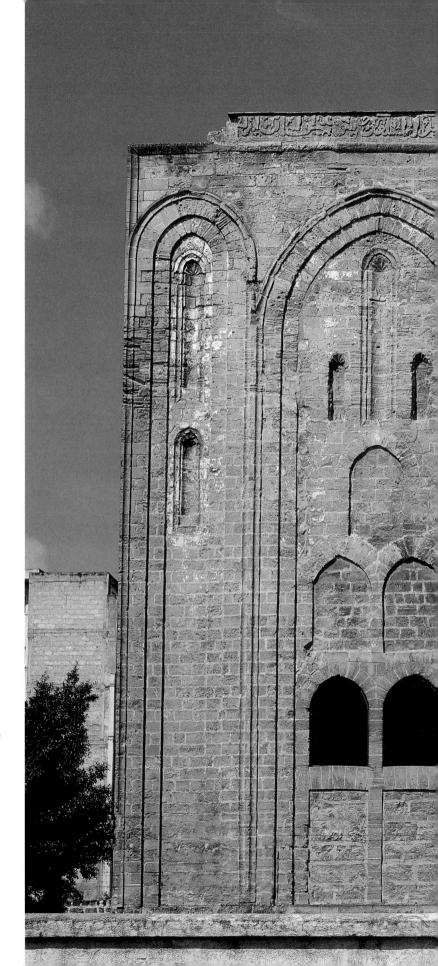

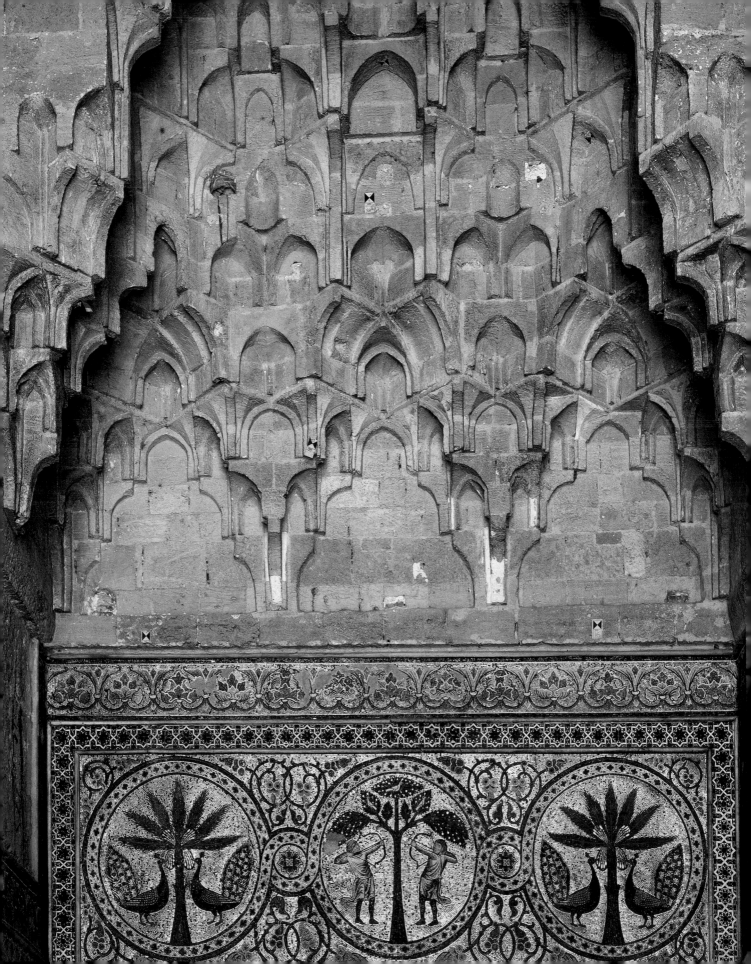

Left:
decorative mosaic strip along the lower wall of the Sala della Fontana della Zisa, Palermo. A seasonal retreat for Norman kings completed between 1165 and 1167, the Castello della Zisa (from the Arab aziz, "splendid") was the most delightful of the so-called "kingly pleasure domes". It was set within a paradisial garden with flowing streams and fishing tanks.

Right:
the cupolas and cloister of San Giovanni degli Eremiti, Palermo.

Page 44:
interior of the Sala delle
Quattro Colonne o dei
Venti, detail, Palazzo dei
Normanni, Palermo.
Along with the Sala
degli Armigeri and the
Sala di Re Ruggero, this
Sala was part of an area
of the palace known as
the Gioaria, from the
Arab al-gawariya – that
is, "the resplendent".

Page 45:
a mosaic lunette in the
Sala di Re Ruggero,
Palazzo dei Normanni,
Palermo. The mosaics,
which date back to the
period between the reign
of William I and
William II (1160-
1170), are an example
of Oriental tastes with
overtones of Islamic
culture. The decorations
on the vault, with
Frederick's eagle, date
from the Swabian
period.

Left:
wooden roof with
aedicules made by Arab
craftsmen in the central
nave of the Cappella
Palatina, detail, Palazzo
dei Normanni, Palermo.

Page 47:
ogival arches dividing
the three naves of the
Cappella Palatina,
detail, Palazzo dei
Normanni, Palermo.

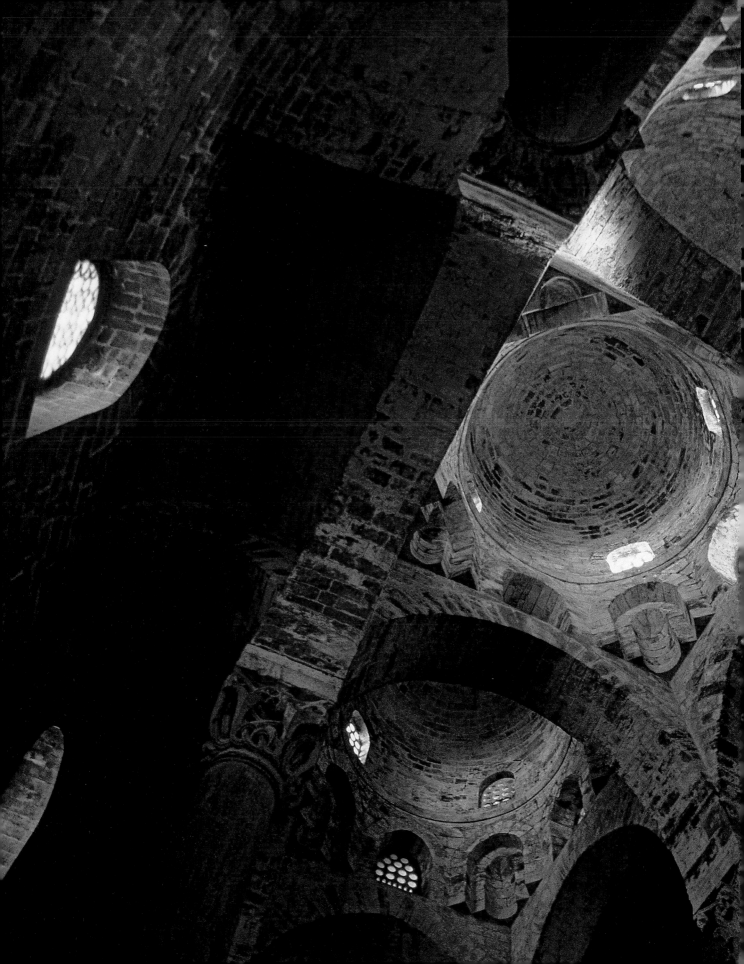

ARAB INFLUENCE

Much has been written about the Arab influence on Sicilian culture. Understandably, very little has remained in the field of architecture – Ruggero d'Altavilla, for example, destroyed 300 mosques in one night when he conquered Palermo. When, however, it came time to rebuild what had been destroyed, the conquerers turned mainly to Arab craftsmen. Their handiwork can be seen in the animal, peacock and geometric motifs – the so-called Arabesques.

Above and left:
cupolas of the church of
San Cataldo, Palermo.

Page 50:
the interior of the church
of Santa Maria
dell'Ammiraglio (or della
Martorana), decorated
with Byzantine-style
mosaics and layered
Baroque decorations,
Palermo.

Page 51:
the Cefalù duomo
(Palermo), founded by
Ruggero II in 1131,
seen from the Rocca.

Mosaic showing Christ the Pantocrator, in the conch of the central apse of the Cefalù duomo (Palermo).

Right:
ogival arches of Arab
derivation, decorated
with geometric motifs
with lava and pumice
stone, Benedictine
monastery cloister,
Monreale duomo
(see pp 92-93).

Page 56:
historiated capitals in
the Benedictine
monastery cloister,
Monreale duomo,
Palermo. The twin
columns are decoarted
with mosaic inlays.

Page 57:
square enclosure with
Oriental-style fountain
in the southern corner of
the Benedictine
monastery cloister,
Monreale (Palermo).

Left:
central nave of the Monreale duomo, Palermo. The conch of the middle apse is dominated by a half-bust of Christ the Pantocrator. The 18 columns that divide the nave are mostly from the Roman period.

Right:
one of the ancient capitals, deftly decorated with clipei of various divinities amongst cornucopias, found on the columns of the naves in the Monreale duomo.

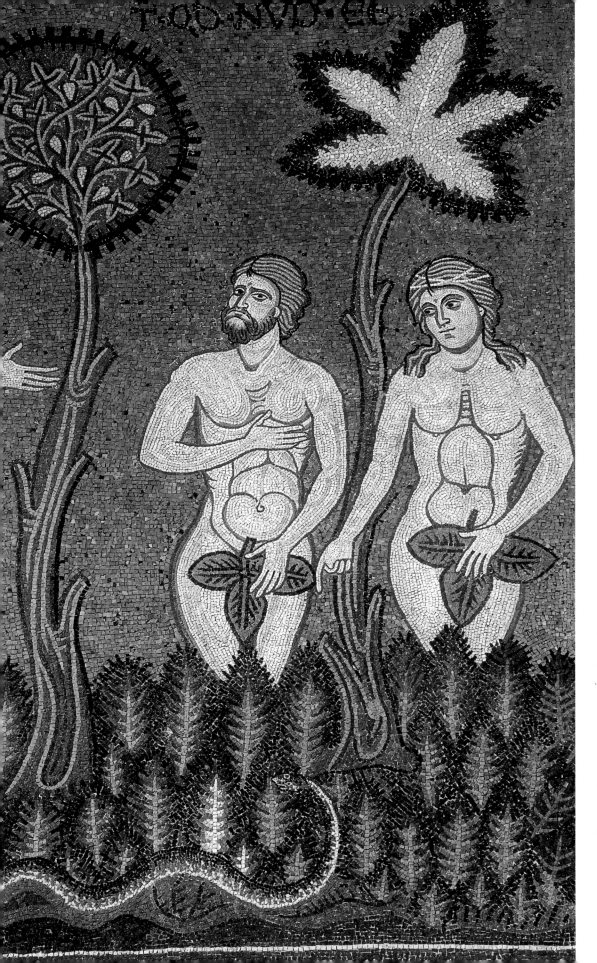

Right:
southern side of the
Palermo duomo.

Page 64:
apse with crossed-arch
decorations, detail,
Palermo duomo. The
apse section of the
duomo has maintained
more of the original
12th-century forms.

Page 65:
detail of the tympanum
over the Gothic-Catalan
portico, by Antonio
Gambara, 1429-1430,
Palermo duomo.

THE CASTLES

Sicily is a land of temples and castles. Even though they were destroyed and rebuilt many times and then abandoned when they were historically superseded, quite a few diverse examples of these ancient fortresses have fortunately remained extant. Some of the most important are the palace-castle of Steri (Palermo), the elevated stronghold at Mussomeli, the ancient Aci Castello complex (rebuilt tens of times) and the delightful Falconara castle which was literally built on the beach. But the most bizzare is probably Sperlinga, whose bottom half has been hollowed out of tufa and upper section built using more traditional methods. When their original function was superseded, many of these constructions were converted to prisons, above all during the reign of the Bourbons.

Preceding page:
normal bridge over the
river Simeto, near
Adrano (Catania).

Right:
the town of Caccamo
(Palermo), dominated by
the crenellated walls of
the Norman castle and
the Norman tower of the
duomo.

Above and adjacent page:
Sperlinga castle (Enna),
built by the Normans
and reinforced by
Frederick II.

Page 72:
interior of Maniace
castle, Syracuse, one of
the most interesting
Swabian castles in Sicily.

Page 73:
the so-called Tower of
Frederick, Enna.

Pages 74-75:
Chiaramonte castle,
Mussomeli
(Caltanissetta).

BAROQUE SICILY

IF THE FRENCH REVOLUTION had come about two centuries earlier, it is very unlikely that the Baroque would have imposed itself with such insolent magnificence in Europe, either in sacred or secular architecture. With its lugubrious thud, the guillotine brought fear to the heart of the crowned heads and the powerful of the time, even those who, far from France, managed to hold onto their crown *and* their head. The artistic and ideological aim of the Baroque was to surprise, to praise the glory not only of the Church but also of an aristocracy who had no intention of hiding their privilege and wealth – on the contrary, they aimed to parade and flaunt.

THE BAROQUE COULD not have hoped to find more fertile terrain than the oligarchic, feudal and extremely Catholic Sicily of the Spanish viceroys. It is certainly not surprising to find it in the larger cities, natural depositories of cathedrals and *palazzi*; but it is astonishing to find it in small towns which are now devoid of political and social importance, and which even in the past, when they did have influence, were merely minute and sparsely populated towns compared to Palermo, Catania, Syracuse or Messina.

NOTO IS PERHAPS the most telling example. The impression a visitor has now is that of a fairly well-off agricultural community which, for reasons which now seem incomprehensible, attracted the attention of a social class that was able to spend as freely as it wanted in order to live and practise its faith. The immense *duomo* staircase seems almost to intimidate. It seems to have been intended to allow two to three thousand people to walk up the steps at the same time; doing it by yourself, slowly, pondering the church's façade, is an experience that certainly leaves its mark. From the top of the staircase, Palazzo Ducezio, which faces the church square, appears to be minuscule. It is rather difficult not to suspect that the architect intended to symbolically draw the line between the dignity of spiritual as opposed to temporal power.

LESS IMPOSING YET NONE the less solemn and numerous are the noble dwellings of Noto, from which the thousands of hectares of land were administered when land and cereals were the basic unit of currency and determined one's real wealth. The most beautiful is Palazzo Villadorata (literally, "golden villa"), a name that almost seems to be taken from a fairy tale, with its long and elaborate balconies held aloft by exquisitely sculpted brackets. You could easily imagine a haughty duchess standing at one of the balconies, flanked by her waiting women. But silence hangs heavy over these 18th-century buildings. Nothing remains of the busy life once lived there by the inhabitants, servants, guards, animal, carriages...

NOTO MIGHT WELL BE a famous centre, but other, smaller towns also hold unexpected surprises. There is Sicli, for example, in the province of Ragusa. The town is nestled in a basin of chalky rock on which the churches, expertly built over what seems to be nothing, dominate the ancient town centre. The houses, huddled together, are built of light-coloured stone, just like the rock they are built on, and their roofs are covered with old roof tiles. In the midst of this apparent poverty there is the grand Palazzo Beneventano. Another example is Naro, in the province of Agrigento, with the island's most original Baroque church. The Church of St Augustine has a tetragonal façade, and a parvis with only four steps and a balustrade ringing the top landing. There are no statues, columns or even a campanile. It does not even seem to be a holy building. It is somewhat similar to the collegiate church of Sortino, in the province of Syracuse. This church is also devoid of the stylistic elements of the Baroque, but then, with its two solitary statues, four columns and small central campanile, it is almost as if the original builder lacked the courage to take the Baroque to its limits.

TWO FURTHER TRULY remarkable examples are to be found in Ibla and Modica. Ibla is ancient Ragusa, a crowded set of winding roads, churches, modest houses, *palazzi* and courtyards that, without any apparent order, have been huddled together on a hill surrounded by a deep narrow valley, beyond which the landscape is as wild and ancient as the town itself.
The *duomo* dominates a small, narrow, sloping piazza, which it would completely cover in its shadow if the sun set just behind it.

MODICA IS MUCH LARGER, and is built on rich, fertile land. Unlike Ibla, the patrician buildings here seem justified; the same can be said about the church of San Pietro. But nothing can adequately prepare the visitor for San Giorgio, which for many is the most beautiful Baroque construction in southern Italy. If the Noto *duomo* is announced by the grandiose staircase, here the church is an apparition. There is no *piazza*, only a narrow road with a church square and 250 steps leading up to the church. You have to raise your head in order to see the turreted façade which, with its two wings topped by a balustrade, gradually tapers off to form the central campanile. It is surrounded by the ancient town buildings – houses, balconies and roofs. The people, it seems, are gathered around their church. And the other campanili seem to keep a respectful distance.

ALTHOUGH MAGNIFICENT, the Sicilian Baroque is only one of the many historical styles that are part of the island's three-thousand-year history. And sometimes two of these styles, from two different eras, come together. This is exactly what happened in Syracuse, where the

Doric temple dedicated to Minerva was incorporated within the 18th-century *duomo.* After you have contemplated the front of the building, take the road to the right of the church. The Greek columns have been given the same function that, in modern architecture, is normally reserved for concrete pilasters, which emerge from the walls. Because they are so large, they can be seen both inside and outside the church. They are all perfectly aligned, except for one solitary pilaster which was thrown seventy centimetres off its axis by the 1542 earthquake. This architectural blend is unique and charged with a symbolic force that even the most distracted tourist cannot help but notice.

THE CITY OF ARCHIMEDE does not simply contain churches, however, but a large number of princely buildings, some of which have been well preserved. These are, for example, Palazzo Beneventano, Palazzo Impellizzeri and Palazzo Senatorio. Enormous courtyards which are now almost devoid of life, stunning wrought-iron railings, and windows protected by centuries-old grilles that seem to have been embroidered, behind which no one stands to observe the walkway outside. But the elegant Syracuse Baroque is in some way "disturbed" by the majestic presence of buildings from other historical periods, making this a city of world-wide importance.

THE STYLES ON DISPLAY in nearby Catania are a lot more coherent. The city almost seems complacent in its dignified and conscious provincialism. Here the thousand-year-old history is quieter, leaving room for traces of a more recent secular and ecclesiastical, though by no means less sumptuous, power. Your first impression is that there seem to be more churches than buildings – and you wouldn't be too wrong. It's almost as if the state decided to respectfully step back and leave more room for the Church. The only magnificent exception is the fable-like Palazzo Biscari. Its terraces are lined with enormous windows surrounded by bas-reliefs which can be clearly seen from the street below. Until a few decades ago, the gulf sea swirled just below the terraces, until the sea was forced back a few hundred metres by urban necessity.

THE CATANIA DUOMO is not the most beautiful church in Sicily, but it certainly ennobles an already extraordinary *piazza*. Piazza Duomo, in fact, with its centrally-located Elephant Obelisk (which has come to symbolise the city), houses Palazzo Uzeda, the seat of local government, with its white outline and laced balconies and windows dotted along the very elegant, dark-grey façade. In the winter months, the expertly-lit piazza will lead you back into the past, bringing forth images and figures from centuries ago. Just like the Benedictine convent, which now houses the city's university. This enormous and articulated complex once housed hundreds of friars, amongst which the frightening romantic figure of Blasco Uzeda, described in Federico de Roberto's *Viceré.*

And, finally, there is Via Crociferi, defined as one of the most beautiful streets in the world. It slopes for a few hundred metres from the gates of the Villa Cerami gardens down to Piazza Dusmet, flanked by steep church squares and the wrought-iron grates of the monasteries. The suggestive nature of this open-air museum of the Baroque has often been used as a cinematic backdrop

for such films as *Bell'Antonio*, based on Vitaliano Brancati's novel, and *Storia di una capinera.*

AS THE CITY'S RESIDENTS well know, Via Crociferi changes with the hour and the seasons; it is fascinating and mystical, but also enigmatic, disquieting and, at times, funereal. Catania's Baroque is definitely an external phenomenon; in Palermo, however, the Baroque has inhabited the décor inside the buildings. Paradoxically, Via Crociferi would still be memorable if there were nothing behind the façades, if the buildings beyond the street had been destroyed and never rebuilt, or worse still rebuilt as blocks of flats and malls. Such is the expressive force of the street.

IN PALERMO, if you want to fully understand what can only be guessed at from the outside, you have to enter the *palazzi* and above all the churches. Two perfect examples are the churches of San Francesco Saverio and Santa Caterina. The initial impression is blinding, almost paralysing – but initial impressions are not enough. You feel you have to photograph the dense swarm of bas-reliefs, marble inlays, sketches, little columns, statues and all sorts of three-dimensional ornamentation and then sit down and calmly study the photo at home. It's almost as if the artist had fallen prey to the writer's syndrome of the blank page: not knowing what to write, he decided to fill every possible blank space along the plastered walls. The effect is an overpowering wealth of detail, where the artist's intention is to stop at nothing in order to surprise the observer.

IN HIS ORATORIOS ESPECIALLY, the stucco maestro Giacomo Serpotta, unlike any other, managed to sublimely hone a deft ability to use ornament without making us privy to his technique, just like prestidigitators only show their public the final, breathtaking effects of their dexterity. Behind this love for the sublime exercising of style there is a Spanish-like passion for form, cultivated and developed not only in architecture, but also in the ceremonial preciosity of language, dress and even pastry, where icings and marzipan are shaped, adorned and painted as if they were stuccos. This reverential love of form sometimes appears to be more

intense than even the spirituality that should have animated the artist's heart and hand.

THIS, IN THE FINAL ANALYSIS, is the greatness of the Baroque. At the same time it constitutes its limit, and is perhaps the reason why, above all in Sicily, this stylistic genre had so many different forms, as if the rules themselves sat too uncomfortably with the island's innate rebelliousness. This can be seen in any number of constructions – from the bizarre church of Sant'Agostino di Naro to the Mazara del Vallo seminary, which is not unlike a Venetian *palazzo*, from the irregular form of the church of Santi Pietro e Paolo in Acireale to the absolute, and at times irrepressible, freedom of private buildings, the most famous (and infamous) of which is surely Villa Palagonia, built by Don Ferdinando Gravina and now in a very parlous state.

FACED WITH THIS APPARENTLY absurd citadel of monstrous forms, Goethe, in his Teutonic rigidity, rebelled and condemned, in his *Italian Journey,* what he considered to be a waste of genius and money, mere manifestations of "a bigoted spirit"

and "disoriented piety". His is an almost psychological interpretation of the recondite thoughts of the artist – and he may not have been wrong.

He didn't for a moment even suspect that poor Don Ferdinando, by hyperbolically emphasising the stylistic defects of the Baroque, was actually trying to display a private and perhaps even painful personal Vesper, a rebellion most certainly not against an architectural canon, but against an ideology of appearances that, for centuries, had constituted the very soul of Sicily and that the arrival of the Spaniards had sanctioned. Hence, even though the so-called Villa dei Mostri (literally the Villa of Monsters) is an almost insignificant element in the island's Baroque, it is none the less fundamental to our understanding of "Sicilianity" and its myriad manifestations.

PALERMO

Before 948 CE, when Palermo became the capital of the Sicilian Emirate and within ten years one of the most important centres of the Arab world, the city was only one of many vying for power on the island. Then Frederick II made it European, but without denying any of its recent history. Decadence set in with the Angevins, continued with the Aragonese, and became chronic with the Bourbons. All of the island's contradictions and complexities are encapsulated in its architecture. Alongside the ignomonies erected during the "building boom" and often directly adjacent to these architectural horrors we find incredibly beautiful examples from the past, veritable revenants, able to surprise the visitor who comes across them for the first time. And Palermo is also the city of the Vespers.

Right:
seen from below, one of the four concave façades surrounding Piazza Vigliena, also known as Quattro Canti, 1609- 1620, Palermo. The piazza, *which is at the crossroads of Corso Vittorio Emanuele and Via Maqueda, constructed by the eponymous Viceroy, is one of the urban replanning projects from the early 17th century.*

Ajacent page:
cupolas of the church of
San Giuseppe dei
Teatini, 1612-1645,
Palermo.

Right:
Pretoria fountain, detail,
Palermo. Made by the
sculptor Francesco
Camilliani between
1554 and 1555 for a
Florentine villa, it was
later sold to the city of
Palermo and placed here
in 1574-1575.

Pages 86-87:
Pretoria fountain, detail,
Palermo. The circular
form of the monument,
built over three tiers,
contains three concentric
tanks decorated by
statues showing pagan
deities, animals, tritons
and mermaids.

Page 88:
marble tarsia and
sculptural group
depicting David and
Abigail, choir of the
church of Gesù (Casa
Professa), Palermo. The
interior decorations,
worked on by many
craftsmen and artists,
make the church one of
the highest examples of
the Sicilian Baroque.
The choir sculptures are
by Gioacchino
Vitagliano.

Page 89:
interior, central floor
plan, with corner
chapels, in the church of
San Francesco Saverio,
Palermo.

Pages 90-91:
altar frontal in mixed
marble, second half of
the 18th century, in the
senatorial chapel of the
Immacolata, church of
San Francesco d'Assisi,
Palermo.

Right:
interior of the Santa
Cita oratory, famous for
Giacomo Serpotta's
stuccoes, 1688-1718,
Palermo.

Left:
"catacombs" of the
Capuchin convent,
detail, Palermo. Along
the corridors of the
convent crypt, from the
17th century to 1881,
the bodies of prelates
and members of the
Palermo nobility would
be laid out according to
their sex, their social
status and their
profession.

Adjacent page:
Fra Matteo Bavera, large
coral lamp, detail,
1633 (Trapani, Museo
Regionale "Peopoli").

THE BAROQUE IN SMALL TOWNS

There are "minor" marvels of the Baroque almost everywhere in Sicily, both in the churches and in the *palazzi*. Sometimes there is only a balcony. The most exquisite example is San Giorgio in Modica, which suddenly comes into view as you approach. But the list of Baroque masterpieces is endless. In the Ragusa district there is the highest concentration of buildings in the Baroque style. Apart from Noto, which deserves a chapter to itself, it is well worth your while visiting Ragusa, Ragusa Ibla, Comiso, Ispica and Scicli, which is reminiscent of an 18th century Neapolitan Christmas manger with its perspective views and sloping structure.

Left:
façade of the church of Madre di Buscemi (Syracuse), mid-18th century.

Right:
interior of the octagonal cupola in the church of Santa Chiara, Alcamo (Trapani), circa 1721.

NOTO

Under Arab rule, Noto was the capital of one of the three districts Sicily was divided up into. Here there is an amazing concentration of Baroque remains, and principally the duomo, whose cupola recently partly caved in, and the Monastero del Salvatore. There are also non-religious examples, such as Palazzo Ducezio, the local government building, and Villa Eleonora and the incredible Palazzo Villadorata (both private buildings), whose ornate balconies look out over a very narrow street that is covered in colourful petals each year for the very popular feast known as the Festa dell'Infiorata.

Page 98:
façade of the church of San Sebastiano, Ferla (Syracuse), detail, 1734-1741.

Right:
tower bell of the Benedictine Monastero del Salvatore, Noto (Syracuse), detail, 1706.

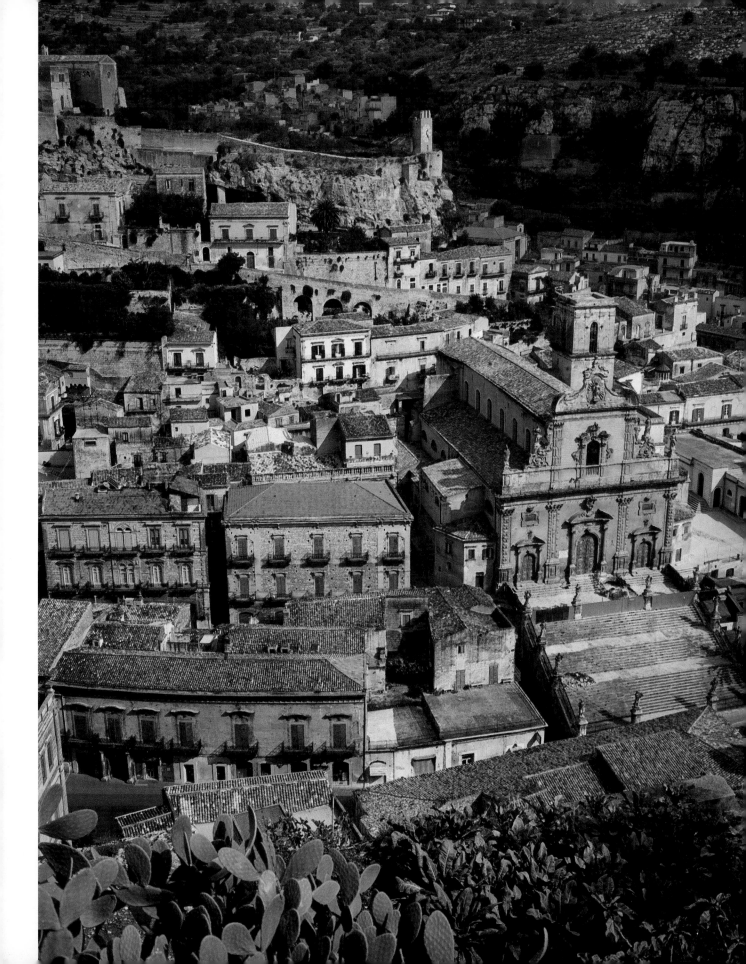

Pages 100-101:
brackets with grotesque
figures holding up the
Baroque balconies of
Palazzo Villadorata,
Noto (Syracuse).

Page 102:
view of Ragusa Ibla. In
the foreground, the
campanile of the church
of Idria, built in 1626
by the Knights of Malta
and rebuilt in 1739.

Page 103:
view of Modica
(Ragusa). On the right,
the monumental
Baroque staircase of the
church of San Pietro.

Left:
Greek columns
incorporated into the
side of the Syracuse
duomo.

Right:
detail of the façade of
the Syracuse duomo,
rebuilt between 1725
and 1753 according to
a design by the architect
Andrea Palma, after the
1693 earthquake
destroyed Val di Noto.

THE BAROQUE *PALAZZI*

Sacred and profane, with Spanish dignity and without vying, they offered themselves to the fearful gaze of the faithful and vassals alike, showing off the power and wealth they represented. Without going as far as the famous Palazzo Villadorata (Noto), Palazzo Beneventano (Syracuse and Scicli), Palazzo Biscari (Catania) and many other authentic monuments of the period, all you needed in a small town was a rounded balcony with the hint of a frieze over the opening to certify your family's social and economic position.

Above:
bracket along the main façade of Palazzo Vermexio, detail, Syracuse.

Right:
Palazzo Beneventano, Scicli (Ragusa).

CATANIA

A splendid provincial town, Catania does not have the architectural grandeur of Palermo or the historical weight of Syracuse, but it does exert its fascination, not least of all because of the cordial and vivacious nature of its inhabitants. The remains of the ancient city are flanked by the regal charm of Palazzo Biscari and the monumental Benedictine monastery. And you cannot go to the *odeon* or the Greek theatre without knowing exactly where they are, tightly surrounded by *palazzi* and almost impossible to get to. Catania may not be the most beautiful city in Sicily, but it certainly is special.

Adjacent page:
the terrace on the
sea-front façade of
Palazzo Biscari.

Right:
Galleria degli Uccelli,
Palazzo Biscari.

*Above and right:
some of the surviving
tufa "monsters" (the
earliest was sculpted in
1747), Villa Palagonia,
Bagheria (Palermo).*

THE FEUDAL SICILY
OF THE GATTOPARDI FAMILY

SICILY'S HAS BEEN a strange destiny. It was here that the first parliament worthy of being labelled as such was founded thanks to the great Swabian Frederick II, whose contemporaries called *stupor mundi*. Here, for about twenty centuries, art and culture expressed the best that Europe has been able to express. And yet the island has never managed to become a real state; nor, consequently, has it ever had its own army to affirm or defend its national identity.

THE TERMS "FIEF" OR "FEUD" were used for the first time in the 9th century, when the general rules were established, even though the concept had always existed. From the Phoenicians' opportunistic settlements along the Mediterranean coast to England's colonisation of India, the conquering and administration of a country and its inhabitants is part of man's history, just as, from the Sicilian Vespers against the Angevins to the American War of Independence against the English, revolt and rebellion are the only means available to break the chains of dominion.

THE CHAINS MAY SEEM pleasant to the tourist, since each dominant force, by imposing its weapons and iniquitous taxes, has none the less left traces of itself, not only within the people and language, but in the architecture, art, literature, culture and farming methods. Owners, emirs, governors, viceroys... the names were always different, sometimes there was a sense of intolerance at the power of the those who had sent them to administer, at times as the blind and self-satisfied instrument of this power.

Beneath them there were vast numbers of vassals whose intention was to gain riches and keep a strangle-hold on the large or small dominion of land and people assigned to them.

IF YOU ABANDON THE CLASSICAL ITINERARY made up of art and sea and move into the centre of Sicily, you can still be surprised by the frequent expanse of land without so much as a village, where the very rare country houses seem to have been abandoned decades ago or have very recently been restructured. This is the traditional Sicily of large swathes of wheat fields, where the sloping hills have been stripped of their trees because no one has

Page 112:
terrace of Villa Valguarnera, Bagheria (Palermo).

Page 113:
Sala Basile, Villa Igiea, detail, Palermo.

bothered to plant them where there weren't any or to replant them after having felled woods and forests for money. These are the effects of feudalism, where thousands of hectares of land were concentrated in the hands of a single lord. This effectively stopped small landowners from using the land; these would certainly have looked after their small properties much better, having to live there themselves.

THE GATTOPARDI FAMILY descended from these old feudal land owners and continued their traditions until World War II and the agrarian reform, which eradicated them. Their castles, abandoned centuries earlier, are now empty husks dominating nothing. But they owned much more than just land. They owned mines, tuna haulers and ships. They lived in the cities. Each town has one or more seigneurial dwellings. But it is Palermo which is the capital of moribund "Gattopardismo". Palazzo Butera, which required hundreds of servants just for everyday maintenance, is where the princes received aristocrats and the crowned heads of Europe. The unforgettable ballroom scene

in Visconti's *Gattopardo* was shot in Palazzo Valguarnara Ganci, in Piazzetta Croce dei Vespri.

MANY OF THESE noble constructions were torn down to make way for blocks of flats in a frighteningly symbolic handing over of power. Others survived, such as Villa Whitaker, Villa Bordonaro (the work of the prolific architectural genius Ernesto Basile) and Villa Caruso. In an era in which travelling was not easy, not even for those with money at their disposal, the month of June was when the Palermo aristocracy spent the Sicilian summer, which Brancati defined as being "as long and bleak as a Russian winter", in their country villas, which were cooler and greener, or in their country residences, which were closed for the rest of the year.

LIKE THEIR CITY *palazzi,* these buildings have paid a heavy price to the financial collapse of their owners and to the fact that they were too large and expensive to maintain. Even if none of the surviving buildings is as famous (or infamous) as the so-called Villa dei Mostri in Bagheria, there are still quite a few "provincial residences" of the last

feudal landowners worthy of a visit. One such example is Palazzo Branciforti in Bagheria. And the magnificent and unusual Villa Eleonora, in Noto. And Donnafugata, in the Ragusa district.

THE DUCEA DI NELSON, on Etna, deserves a visit. The castle was donated by the Bourbons to the English admiral as thanks for his support.
The place is fascinating and a unique experience. But it is also an exemplary tale of how a Sicilian castle and lands were donated by a French sovereign, living in Naples, to an English citizen who did not live there, and whose administrators turned it into an inviolable national enclave on foreign soil before which even Garibaldi's men were forced to retreat.

THE OPPOSITE IS TRUE for Palermo's Villa Igiea, which takes the name of Esculapius' wife, the goddess of health and wellbeing. It is now a luxury hotel and a very special place for an aperitif amongst the palms and mosaics, even though the Florio family had it built not for the family but as a free river-side sanatorium for tuberculosis sufferers. The

Florios were a splendid Gattopardi dynasty who gave their name to the Marsala wine produced in the large vineyards of western Sicily and the famous Targa car race which, weather permitting, drew crowds of up to 400,000 spectators.

IN THE LAND OF MYTH, even the Gattopardi family became a myth. So much, in fact, that it is hard to tell where reality ends and legend begins. Their feats were not sung in public squares like those of the champions of liberty, but, whether they were good or bad deeds, they were communicated orally. And some of the characters involved were quite bizarre. There was Prince Manganelli from Catania, for example, who loathed Rome's government and refused to pay any taxes. When his furniture was confiscated and taken into the square to be auctioned off, he would come onto his balcony, wait for the last bid to be made for the pieces, and raise the bid to exactly what the tax collectors demanded. He would then send the money down with a servant and order the officiating authorities to bring his furniture back upstairs. His taxes were settled for another year.

AND THEN THERE WAS Baron Lombardo of Canicattì, who, when faced with a delegation of fellow citizens, hat in hand, asking him to offer his harvest for the families of those who had died in the Battle of Adua in Africa, looked daggers at them and refused. "I am Baron Lombardo," he said. "You cannot come here and demand charity as you've done with others. When you've finished harvesting, come back and tell me how much you've harvested – and I'll give you twice as much again." And the Princess of Trabia, who had her table laid with solid gold plates and cutlery. And like many others, all of whom displayed excessive amounts of generosity, dissipation, extroversion, depression, chauvinism or misanthropy.

HIDDEN AMONGST THE MANY concealed or at least camouflaged citizens of the island's numerous characters, there is a special Sicily, proud of its great traditions. A Sicily made of Albanians who arrived around the mid-15th century fleeing the ever-expanding Ottoman Empire. These immigrants originally founded nine towns, only a day's horse ride from each other.

Only two or three still maintain their original traditions, or as much tradition as the third millennium allows.
But even if their language, food, customs, pride and many other things beside have been lost or are being lost, the urban structure still reveals the noble and indomitable warlike and tribal spirit that originally inspired these little towns.

PALAZZO ADRIANO, in the extreme south of the province of Palermo, is a town made up of three small strongholds which all lead into a central square where two churches, one Catholic and the other of Byzantine-Greek-Catholic extraction, face each other. For centuries, the houses of each stronghold were linked to each other by doors that were never opened. Thus, in case of enemy attack, it would have taken much more than just breaking down one door to exterminate a family.
The family would, in the meantime, have fled to the adjoining house. There are very few cross streets here, the idea having been to keep the town as compact as possible. Along the main roads, with their exquisite Byzantine paving with geometric patterns, the walls form little niches where armed citizens would hide to attack their enemy from behind.

THE LITTLE TOWN was surrounded by a wall with a series of doors and gates, each dedicated to a Madonna whose frescoed image could be found on the adjoining wall. It must have been like living in a military camp, constantly on guard against possible invasions that, luckily for Europe, never took place. This sense of impending attack created, amongst people from another land who shared an intensely-experienced language and religion, a solidarity that is hard to imagine nowadays. Until only a few decades ago, a flat stone would be placed in each vegetable and fruit orchard, which could not be fenced in for any reason. If poor people walked past and wanted to pick some fruit, they would take as much as they wanted. But if anyone who wasn't really poor did so, they would leave some money on the stone for the owner. And no one except the owner would ever dream of taking the money. This, too, seems to be a myth. But it isn't.

THE FIEFS OF THE DUKES OF BRANCIFORTE

You would have to spend a long time indeed ferreting through the State Archives if you wanted to identify all the land owned by the Branciforte family, even though they had a bas-relief map sculpted over the entrance door to their reception halls to show their main fiefs. These included Barrafranca, Militello Val di Catania, Butera and Mazzarino, for a total of tens of thousands of hectares.

Adjacent page:
sea-front façade of
Palazzo Branciforte
Butera, Palermo.

Below:
map of Mazzarino,
showing the lands owned
by the Branciforte family,
Palazzo Branciforte
Butera, Palermo.

THE LANDED ESTATES

Landed estates go back thousands of years in Italy, and they only became fiefs in the strict historical sense after the fall of the Roman Empire, when the lands were handed over to the notability of the invading hordes. It might be defined as a large tract of land which is little cultivated, partly uncultivated and partly leased out. In the South, and particularly in Sicily, this led to great social inequality, eventually culminating in abject poverty and revolts, which in turn led to the occupation of land and the agrarian reform which abolished feudal land laws in 1812. This was far too late to make up for the social catastrophe brought about by inured abuse and submission.

Left:
agrarian landscape near Valguarnera (Enna).

Adjacent page:
agrarian landscape in the Piana di Catania.

A typical agrarian scene in the interior, with low stone fences and grazing goats.

DONNAFUGATA

Even though it is mentioned as a summer holiday location for Prince Salina in Tomasi di Lampedusa's *Il Gattopardo*, the Donnafugata in the Ragusa district has nothing to do with the imaginary Donnafugata described by di Lampedusa. This is a large, 19th-century castle, now owned by the local council, with a beautiful, elegant façade and a light Neogothic loggia.

Adjacent page: small temple in the gardens of Castello di Donnafugata, Ragusa.

Right: Neogothic loggia, Castello di Donnafugata, Ragusa.

THE WHITAKERS AND NELSON'S DUCHY

The sons and heirs of Benjamin Ingham, a genial merchant gentleman (who brought marsala wine to Great Britain), the Whitakers were introduced to the Sicily that mattered as *bona fide* Sicilians, enamoured of the land they enriched and that made them wealthy. They were anti-Bourbonic, patrons and protectors of the arts; they were cultivated and had an eye for the society that surrounded them. In 1799, Ferdinand I gave Horatio Nelson a large estate and the title of Duke of Bronte. It seems that the future victor of the Battle of Trafalgar graciously accepted both the land the touch of Sicilian-ness that this bestowed upon him.

*Adjacent page:
entrance to the main
façade of Villa Whitaker,
Palermo.*

*Right:
castello di Nelson,
Bronte (Catania).*

ART NOUVEAU

A long, lively avenue was opened in Palermo in 1900. This was Via Liberty (the Italian for "Art Nouveau"), and the marvellous Art-Nouveau villas that flank the entire avenue represented the latest contest between the aristocratic families of Palermo to show that they, too, were in step with a new style that was being imported from France. The style was light, capricious and elegant, the ideal for a social class that was perpetually bored and hungry for novelties. Now, almost all of those buildings have been lost. Ironically, the family that best interpreted Art Nouveau had no coat of arms at all – the Florio family. Their home in Viale Regina Margherita and Villa Igiea, along the seaside, continue to bear the family name.

THE FEUDAL SICILY OF THE GATTOPARDI FAMILY • 133

Left:
Art-Nouveau entrance
door, Canicattini Bagni
(Syracuse).

Adjacent page:
mosaic Art-Nouveau sign
for the Morello bakery,
Capo market, Palermo.

SICILY'S SEA,
ISLANDS AND VOLCANOES

MYTHS, LEGENDS, popular traditions and fables certainly have the upper hand compared with reality when you leave behind things, objects and history books in favour of the sea, the islands and volcanoes. And the Greeks have had quite a lot to do with this great heritage. If the original Homeric Ulysses never really existed (but who can tell?), many others, whose names have been swallowed by history and the sea before their stories could be told, have travelled either out of choice or necessity and dreamt of *nostos,* their return home. What moved them to travel towards an inviting and frightening Unknown was a thirst for knowledge in its most primitive form: migrating in search of new worlds to colonise, conquer or simply visit.

Is PANTELLERIA PERHAPS Calypso's fabulous island where Ulysses stopped, first as a guest then seduced by Calypso, the daughter of Ocean and Thetis? Many Homer scholars have affirmed as much. It is on this volcanic island that Africa and Europe have celebrated and consummated their millenarian marriage. And many place-names are proof of this – Balata dei Turchi,

Mount Gelkhamar, Cala Gadir. Were the Aci Trezza stacks really hurled into the ocean by a furious Cyclops? A nice thought, though not that easy to believe. It would be a lot simpler for the island's ancient inhabitants and its visitors to believe that Vulcan, in the depths of Etna, was helped by Cyclops to forge Zeus' lightning bolts.

EVEN MODERN, positivist minds are struck by such thoughts – try visiting the active crater of Etna, which the local inhabitants simply call *a muntagna,* The Mountain. There are no cliffs or steep walls to climb. Simply an interminable, sometimes gentle, slope that slowly rises through small towns and pine forests until you reach desolate stretches of thorny bush, sporadic tufts of grass and, finally, a totally grey landscape. Up there, everything is covered with lava dust, even the preceding winter's snow. Everything is conserved with the same substance the Romans and Arabs used to cool their wine or make sherbet in summer. As you climb, you come across large swathes of damp earth, and if you remove the earth with your hands you will soon come across last year's snow.

Page 138:
view of Etna from Taormina (Messina). In the foreground, Badia Vecchia, Norman turrets, restored in the 14th century.

Page 139:
a popular figurehead on a fishing boat.

AT THREE THOUSAND METRES there is no sign of either vegetable or animal life. If there are any clouds, they are below you, and not over your heads. But if it's a clear day, you can see as far as Costa dei Saraceni and even Syracuse, a landscape which, during the summer months, lies sweltering in 40-degree heat, while up here you have to keep your windcheater on. The central crater, which has been dormant for a long time, is a dizzying vortex, and only expert Alpine climbers have the courage to face it and imagine it during one of its fiery outbursts.

BUT THERE IS NOTHING that will prepare you for the brief excursion to the edges of the active crater, led by an Alpine guide wearing the typically Sicilian flat cloth cap, the *coppola*. The bitter sulphuric smoke gushes out of the crater and the constant, violent roar that accompanies it incites a terror that has nothing of the modern or positivistic about it.
It's not very reassuring to know that there is no divine blacksmith down there; nor is it very reassuring to feel a primordial force that at any moment might erupt and cover anything with lava, destroying anything that man has ever dared build.

FOR THE PEOPLE OF THE PERIOD, Scylla and Carybdis, the devourers of sailors, must have been no less monstrous. These were hollow cliffs that swallowed and disgorged water, the demonic sovereigns of the Messina Straits, where the extremities of the island and peninsula almost meet (in some geological prehistory they were probably joined together). Originally, there were probably strong cross-currents in the area, and these were in all probability dangerous for the flimsy vessels of the time. Hence, any crossing of that part of the sea was transformed into a nightmare. Scylla and Carybdis are not very far from magical Tindari, an ancient Greek settlement and shrine. From high atop the cliff the sea below looks like an atoll, where the soft moving sands represent a coral reef, unique within the Mediterranean. Here Scylla and Carybdis, actually quite close, seem as distant as the era in which their myth was born.

FURTHER NORTH there are Stromboli and Vulcano. Vulcano, according to myth, was one of the many furnaces, along with Etna and Lemnos, inhabited by the unhappy god Vulcan. Unlike Etna, Stromboli, which is the only permanently active volcano in Europe, is not poised on a large island, but recent lava flows have left deep cliffs that jut dramatically into the ocean below. Here two primordial elements, fire and water, engage in almost daily battle and, when the battle takes place in the dead of night, the spectacle allows us to imagine what the beginning of creation might have been like.

THE ENTIRE ARCHIPELAGO of the Aeolian Islands takes its name from the god that commanded the winds and gave Ulysses (yes, him again) a series of goatskins containing some of the god's capricious creatures. When Ulysses' crew inadvertently let them loose all together, they unleashed a storm that destroyed the small fleet before Ulysses' dream of returning to Ithaca could come true. Myth and history once again merge to the west, in the Egadi archipelago, where in 241 BCE, the Consul Catullus, who had just beaten the formerly invincible Carthaginian fleet, made

the voice of Rome ring out in the Mediterranean. This, for the enterprising and wealthy city of Carthage, was a foretaste of other defeats.

ACCORDING TO LIVY, Carthage's defeat was ensured thanks to the bronze rostra placed at the prow of the Roman triremes, which, after having shafted the enemy vessels, ensnared them and allowed the strong Roman infantry to board the craft and engage in direct battle. But perhaps this is all just a legend, like the legend regarding the siege of Syracuse, the final conquest of which was held off by the genius of Archimedes, whose mirrors and enormous articulated beams allowed the Syracusans to burn and destroy the Roman ships that had anchored along the city walls of Ortigia. A very unlikely occurrence, considering the limited technical knowledge of the period. However, the Consul Marcellus must have had good reason to spare the mathematician's life the day the city fell. Archimedes was eventually killed by an anonymous legionary.

THE SOFT BREEZE OF MYTH made itself felt for quite a while in

Syracuse, and it has brought us the story of Arethusa, a nymph much loved by Artemis, who turned her into a spring to save her from being raped. The spring can still be seen today, adorned by papyri just a few metres from the sea. Quite a way inland, however, along the banks of Lake Pergusa, another violent attempt was thwarted when Hades managed to take Persephone away from her devoted mother Demeter and lead her, in the guise of a queen, to the kingdom of the dead. Today, the lake's natural amphitheatre, surrounded by a racing car circuit, seems overcrowded with holiday houses and restaurants, but 19th century travellers talk of its almost supernatural, almost threatening, silence. They stated that the place was deserted even by birds, as if in memory of Demeter's lamentations and her shouting at the still waters to give her back her daughter. This, they say, is why the area is surrounded by a heavy atmosphere of pain and respectful silence.

THE SICILIAN SEA is changeable. Anyone who has sailed around the island has the impression of having visited many countries at once. The windmills of the Trapani salt mines, the tropical oasis at Vendicari in the province of Syracuse, the basalt reefs of Catania and the spread of beaches to the south, from the spectral petrochemical works of Gela, which look like an immense alien spaceship incapable of taking flight, to the eternal colonnades of the Temple of Concord in Agrigento. And beyond Agrigento, in the small town of Realmonte, there are the spectacular "Turkish steps", a guileless set of clay and limestone steps that lead down to the sea, a handy anchoring spot for the Saracen pirates who would then walk up the steps onto the mainland on the lookout for booty and women.

THE SICILIAN SEA is beautiful, and yet terrifying. Above all for animals, as can be gleaned from the nets and equipment used in the last of the Sicilian tuna-fishing industries in Favignana, and the fishing trawlers used for swordfish in the Straits. Men, however, are no less threatened, and they have feared the sea for millennia. Landing at Punta Raisi airport in Palermo at night, during a storm, is an experience that can only be savoured once you're safely ensconced in a car driving away from the airport. Close by and invisible, the Mediterranean hurls itself against the breakwaters, producing an endless deafening roar which transmits a vague sense of panic, as if at any moment a solid wall of water might materialise and destroy everything in its wake. This is the booming voice of Poseidon, reasserting his authority over the waves. Scylla and Carybdis are far away, but the primitive fear and superstition that created them is still present, lying dormant within each and every one of us.

A TREASURE OF ISLANDS

Nature has circumscribed Sicily with a crown of islands that the ancients thought was a gift from and the house of the gods. In the Aeolian and Lipari Islands lived Aeolus, the mythical god of the winds who gave Ulysses his windbag. The Cyclopes lived on Vulcano; Vulcan had his furnace here as well. In the middle of the Channel of Sicily there is "an imaginary island" – the legendary Ferdinandaea which appears and disappears, and which the English claim as theirs.

*Pages 144-145:
the rocky promontory known as the Arch of the Elephant, Pantelleria (Trapani), the largest of the islands surrounding Sicily and whose name in Arab means "daughter of the winds".*

*Left:
the island of Stromboli, in the Aeolians (Messina), viewed from the little island of Strombolicchio.*

*Right:
the stacks of Scopello (Trapani).*

Pages 148-149:
a panoramic view of the
islands of Salina, Lipari
and Vulcano in the
Aeolians, from Filicudi
(Messina).

Pages 150-151:
the castle on the island
of Lipari (Aeolians,
Messina).

Right:
home with bougainvillea
on the island of Linosa
(Agrigento).

Pages 154-155:
a section of the coast
near Cala Rossa on the
island of Favignana
(Trapani), with entrance
to the tufa quarries.

THE SALT PANS

Between Marsala and Trapani there is a long stretch of coastline that looks like a chessboard of garish colours – these are the salt pans, and their colours go from the light pink seen at dawn to blue in the bright daylight and a warm orange at sunset. Once, the sea gave man everything he needed, including salt... Today, all that's left are the remnants of those places, the remains of backbreaking hardship that have been transformed into breathtaking beauty.

Left:
salt pans on the islands of Stagnone, near Mozia (Trapani).

Right:
the windmill of the Ettore salt pan near Mozia (Trapani).

Pages 158-159:
the Nubia salt pans near Paceco (Trapani), with the Egadi islands in the background.

Pages 160-161:
mule being used for threshing, island of Pantelleria (Trapani).

TUNA FISHING

Each year large shoals of tuna fish migrate through the sea of Sicily as they head north and then south again. Fishermen get ready for the catch by putting together their tuna nets – a series of rectangular net "chambers" which lead to the "chamber of death" with its very fine, tight netting. When the tuna have been "channeled" into this last chamber, the fishermen ready themselves for the slaughter – a savage rite that must be endured if man is to survive.
Royal families from the rest of Europe would once come to Sicily especially to view the slaughter.

Pages 162-163:
a recent scene of the
slaughter of tuna fish,
Favignana (Trapani).

Above
and right:
two scenes from the
frightening ritual.

THE VOLCANOES

Sicily lives under the sign of fire: Etna, the Aeolian islands, Ustica, Pantelleria and Linosa represent eleven volcanoes above sea level, but there are many more that lie submerged, surrounding Sicily. Every now and then they erupt – sometimes with flows of incandescent lava, sometimes with showers of red-hot lapilli. They are overbearing presences that man has tried to exorcise with myth, superstition and religious faith.

Right:
the island of Vulcan, the Aeolians, seen from the top of a volcanic stack.

Page 168:
fumaroles on the crater of the island of Vulcano.

Page 169:
the volcanic scoria along the slopes of the volcano on the island of Stromboli.

Left:
sulphur fumaroles on the
crater of a volcanic stack,
island of Vulcano
(Aeolians, Messina).

Right:
the harsh, inhospitable
winter landscape along
the slopes of Etna, near
Randazzo (Catania).

Pages 172-173:
a frightening,
close-range image of
a lava flow.

SICILY AND ITS FEASTS

THE OLDER A FEAST, the easier it is to identify its ancient origins in religion, and you don't need great imaginative skills to travel back in time to when animistic paganism assumed a thousand different forms to help govern the fears felt by primitive cultures. Gods were given human, animal or phantasmagorical faces; yet none of them ever smiled or had a kind word for man who, in order to respect or venerate them, needed to fear them.

NO ONE HAS EVER COUNTED the number of divinities that have been lost in Sicily, either forgotten or prohibited by ecclesiastical authority. Nor would it be worth anyone's while, considering that hundreds have survived, all loved, venerated and financially backed by popular enthusiasm, often with visible gifts in the form of expensive gifts or hard cash pinned to the *vara,* that is a dais in honour of Christ, the Virgin or a saint, often borne by members of a confraternity or simple followers who enthusiastically embrace the opportunity (and sometimes danger) of carrying so obvious a symbol of faith.

APART FROM THE LARGE FEASTS dedicated to patron saints, most of the feasts are in honour of Good Friday (representing mourning, grief and expiation) and Easter (resurrection, joy and reconciliation).

THE GOOD FRIDAY PROCESSIONS are held in the evening or at night, and are sad, sometimes lugubrious, affairs held to the accompaniment of torches, music and wailing. Needless to say, they are dramatically suggestive. Each town has its own variations. At Collesano, hooded figures set out at dawn. In Marsala there is a procession of so-called "Veronicas", veiled women wearing family jewels and Byzantine costumes. In Ganci, ancient costumes are also worn by members of various confraternities on Palm Sunday. Sixteen *vare* dating back to the late 19th century are carried aloft in Caltanissetta.

THE CHARACTERISTIC PERSONALITIES on these occasions are the so-called *Sanpaolini,* papier-mâché simulacra of the saints and apostles worn by particularly robust followers who look out from a little grille positioned at the height of the

Page 174:
market stall selling roasted seeds. The decorations are the work of the Ducato family, famous cart painters from Bagheria (Palermo).

Page 175:
statue of St Lucy, Syracuse. The statue is put on public display only on the saint's feast day.

simulacrum's stomach. Unlike the *vare,* which represent the stations of Christ's Passion, the *Sanpaolini,* often arbitrary and carnival-like, have never been accepted by the Church, which has sometimes intervened in an attempt to suppress them. Popular revolt has ensued.

EVEN MORE PAGAN are the devils of Prizzi, three demons in grotesque masks who dance until others dressed as angels symbolically kill them with swords. Apart from Easter, another particularly popular feast is the one dedicated to St Joseph. In the town of Salemi they make loaves of bread in the shape of objects, fruit and animals, and in the evening there is a banquet for the poor (a common custom in many other towns). In lots of towns, live "mangers" are organised each Christmas. In Alcara Li Fusi the saint's *vara* is carried by women, which is contrary to the tradition in the rest of Sicily.

IN MAZZARINO IN MAY, a very heavy float carrying the so-called "Christ of Olmo" is heaved onto the shoulders of bare-footed hooded carriers who are naked under their cloak. From balconies along the route, the faithful throw garlands of yellow daisies which eventually cover the entire *vara*. This is a joyous feast which recalls ancient feasts dedicated to Spring in archaic societies.

BUT THE TWO MOST IMPORTANT SICILIAN feasts, in terms of importance and shere numbers, are those dedicated to Santa Rosalia in Palermo and Stant'Agata in Catania. To the former is dedicated a sanctuary in a grotto on Monte Pellegrino, where the saint lived as a hermit and the walls of which are literally covered with silver votive offerings. According to tradition, it was thanks to Rosalia's intercession that the 1624 plague was brought to an end, and since then each year, between the 9th and 14th of July, the large float dedicated to the saint is carried through Palermo, arguably the most disenchanted city in the Mediterranean, followed by an affection that must surprise the inhabitants themselves.

THE CROWDS IN CATANIA, however, are even larger. For three whole days citizens and visitors remember and celebrate their saint, whose martyrdom goes back much further than Rosalia, to the third century

CE. A bust of the saint, completely covered with gems and baubles, actually contains the very few relics of the saint. But the young, unfortunate Agata, like so many other names in the calendar, is above all a symbol. Was it her intransigent refusal to relinquish her virginity to a Roman proconsul that fired Catania's imagination?

IF SO, THEN IT'S NOT SURPRISING that over the following centuries both the Arab and Spanish cultures, both of which were so obsessed with feminine virtue, reinforced the cult of the martyred girl. After all, for a simple illiterate community of almost two thousand years ago, it must have been a lot more simple and instinctive to identify with the suffering of a persecuted girl whose breasts had been amputated than with the Church Fathers' cultivated and supercilious grandeur or the superhuman heroics of the proto-Christian martyrs.

IT IS VERY DIFFICULT to describe in mere words what happens during the two most important moments of the feast. On February 4th, in the dead of night, the people begin to flock to the cathedral. There are literally thousands of people, of all ages, each and every year, and regardless of the weather. The altar is surrounded by a multitude of devoted followers dressed in white who lift the saint's shrine and hold it up to the faithful. The solemnity of the occasion is almost disconcerting.

THE FOLLOWERS, their faces not always very reassuring, shamelessly give vent to their tears; their emotion infects the crowd, who seem to tremble collectively. The culminating moment begins, and the so-called "Dawn Mass" starts. Then the procession leaves the cathedral, slowly making its way through the crowded piazza to Porta Uzeda, where it comes to a stop under the arches of the Marina. The sun is rising, and as soon as its rays hit the bejewelled bust of the saint there is a burst of light that is reminiscent of a silent and peremptory divine message.

THE FOLLOWING NIGHT the float, followed by tens of thousands, does the rounds of the entire city before beginning its climb up the almost impossible slope of Via Sangiuliano. The slope is so steep that the float carriers often have to run towards it in order to reach the top without coming to stop. Once they've got to the top, the *vara* turns into Via Crociferi, where thousands of people have been patiently waiting. The sun hasn't yet fully risen, but there is a sense of foreboding as Sant'Agata comes to a stop in front of the convent of San Benedetto. This is the only day of the year in which the cloistered nuns can leave their convent. The mother superior comes out, offers a bouquet of flowers to the saint and is also given flowers in return.

THEN THERE IS THE MIRACLE. A small group of nuns begin to sing a hymn, without microphones or amplifiers. How many people are there in Via Crociferi? Ten thousand? Twenty thousand? If each of them were to shut their eyes, they would feel they were the only ones there, that the nuns were singing exclusively for them. The crowd is perfectly silent, and the hymn can be heard from one end of the street to the other. In that surreal silence no amount of atheism or agnosticism, however well developed, can protect you from the flood of emotion.

THEN THE HYMN DIES DOWN, and as dawn breaks the darkness, the nuns return to their cloistered life and the young virgin martyr is accompanied once more into the church. The feast comes to a close yet again.

LOCAL FEASTS

A land that has lived
for millenia with
different forms of
upheaval cannot but
interpret these events
as anything other than
divine intervention.
As a consequence, it
is inevitable that a
series of extremely
popular annual feasts
and public displays
should have
developed in Sicily.
These feasts are a
mixture of the sacred
and the profane,
revealing an intensely
passionate nature.

Right:
the procession with
the Vara (a votive cart)
during the feast of
St Sebastian, Cerami
(Enna).

THE HOLY WEEK RITUAL

Of the most suggestive popular celebrations, those held during Holy Week are arguably the most intensely emotional. On the Sunday before Easter there is a joyous Procession of the Palms; the climax, however, comes on Good Friday with the dramatic mystery of the Procession of the Dead Christ. Women wear lavishly embroidered traditional costumes; and men throughout the island dress just as opulently.

Pages 182-183:
the Palm Sunday
procession, Piana delgi
Albanesi (Palermo).

Right:
the Good Friday giudei*,*
Sanfratello (Messina).

Pages 186-187:
the Good Friday cerca*,*
Collesano (Palermo).

Right:
hooded Good Friday
procession marchers,
Enna.

*Above and right:
the Devil and Death at
the Easter celebrations,
Prizzi (Palermo).*

*Pages 194-195:
two surprising scenes
from the St Paul
celebrations, Palazzolo
Acreide (Syracuse).*

Above:
the Assumption vara,
Randazzo (Catania) on
the slopes of Etna.

Right:
the Mastro di Campo
feast, Mezzojuso
(Palermo).